NEW BOOKS FOR NEW READERS

Judy Cheatham
General Editor

KENTUCKY FOLKLORE

R. Gerald Alvey

THE UNIVERSITY PRESS OF KENTUCKY

The New Books for New Readers project was made possible through funding from the National Endowment for the Humanities, the Kentucky Humanities Council, and *The Kentucky Post*. The opinions and views expressed in this book are not necessarily those of the Kentucky Humanities Council.

Scholarly publisher for the Commonwealth,
serving Bellarmine College, Berea College, Centre
College of Kentucky, Eastern Kentucky University,
The Filson Club, Georgetown College, Kentucky
Historical Society, Kentucky State University,
Morehead State University, Murray State University,
Northern Kentucky University, Transylvania University,
University of Kentucky, University of Louisville,
and Western Kentucky University.

Editorial and Sales Offices: Lexington, Kentucky 40508-4008

Library of Congress Cataloging-in-Publication Data
Alvey, R. Gerald, 1935-
    Kentucky folklore / R. Gerald Alvey.
        p. cm.— (New books for new readers)
    ISBN 0-8131-0902-7
1. Folklore—Kentucky. 2. Folklore—Appalachian Region. 3. Oral
tradition—Kentucky. 4. Oral tradition—Appalachian Region.
5. Kentucky—Social life and customs. 6. Appalachian Region—Social life
and customs. 7. Readers for new literates.
I. Title. II. Series.
GR110.K4A48   1989
398'.09769—dc20   89-38083

Contents

Foreword

The New Books for New Readers project was made possible through funding from the National Endowment for the Humanities, the Kentucky Humanities Council, and *The Kentucky Post*. The co-sponsorship and continuing assistance of the Kentucky Department for Libraries and Archives and the Kentucky Literacy Commission have been essential to our undertaking. We are also grateful for the advice and support provided to us by the University Press of Kentucky. All these agencies share our commitment to the important role that reading books should play in the lives of the people of our state, and their belief in this project has made it possible.

The Kentucky Humanities Council recognizes in the campaign for adult literacy a cause closely linked to our own mission, to make the rich heritage of the humanities accessible to all Kentuckians. Because the printed word is a vital source of this heritage, we believe that books focused on our state's history and culture and written for adults who are newly learning to read can help us to serve a group of Kentucky's citizens not always reached or served by our programs. We offer these books in the hope that they will be of value to adult new readers in their quest, through words, for an understanding of what it means to be human.

Ramona Lumpkin, Executive Director
Kentucky Humanities Council

Acknowledgments

This book has been produced with support from the National Endowment for the Humanities, the Kentucky Humanities Council, the Kentucky Literacy Commission, and the University Press of Kentucky. I also wish to thank Joyce Toliver, the coordinator, and all the other people at the Pendleton County Adult Reading Program for their suggestions and editorial assistance: Mark Blanton, E. D., Bobbie Gay, Lois Gibbons, Rex Howard, Lewis Hulley, Judy Miles, Jeff Reinzan, Virginia Shotwell, and Loretta Simpson. Finally, I thank my wife, Donna, a teacher of young people for many years, who read the manuscript and offered suggestions to improve its readability level.

Introduction

This book is about folk culture and folklore in Kentucky. Before talking about folk culture, we need to understand what culture is. Culture is a body of knowledge shared by a group of people. It is also how they learn or acquire that knowledge and how they express that knowledge with one another. Culture includes the way people talk, dress, cook, eat, and act. Culture includes people's beliefs about God and the supernatural, and how they view themselves and other people. Culture also includes all the material objects people create, such as barns, fences, houses, quilts, and musical instruments.

Lifestyle is a current term that means almost the same thing as culture. But culture includes many more things than a lifestyle. Also, people usually *choose* their lifestyle when they become adults. People do not choose their culture. People *learn* their culture from the time they are born. People learn how to talk, act, etc.—how to live—from family, friends, and others around them as they grow up. Often, people are not even aware that they are learning their culture.

In general, culture is the way people learn to live their lives. There are three kinds of culture in

Kentucky and the rest of the United States: elite, popular, and folk culture.

Elite culture is the official, formal culture. You learn elite culture in schools, in churches, from the government, or from any official, formal source. For example, when teachers tell students to say "I do not have any" instead of "I ain't got none," they are teaching the students elite culture.

Elite culture has many rules and guidelines. These rules are rigid, and we must follow them. For example, when a doctor prescribes a medicine, we must take it at exact times so it will work. When the government passes tax laws, we must obey them or we will be fined or sent to jail.

The main purpose of elite culture is to help people to be better human beings, to live better lives, and to make the world a better place. In fact, the reason you are reading this book, learning to read, and learning to think about these things is all part of elite culture. You will be better because of these things.

Popular culture is the second kind of culture in Kentucky and the rest of the United States. Unlike elite culture, we do not learn popular culture in schools. We learn popular culture from TV, radio, newspapers, magazines, movies, and commercials.

For example, from popular culture we learn what brand of deodorant is "manly," what kind of detergent to use for the whitest, brightest clothes, and which pill will cure our headaches the quickest.

Generally, popular culture is commercial culture. Popular culture, for the most part, exists to make money. In order to make lots of money, popular culture must appeal to many people. It must also change constantly, because people want to buy whatever is new or trendy or the "in" thing. Therefore, popular culture does not last very long. Popular culture is faddish. It's here today and gone tomorrow.

Hairstyles and clothing styles are good examples of how popular culture changes. The girl's ponytail and boy's duck tail hairstyles of the 1950s are not worn much today. Nor do you see the Farrah Fawcett hairstyle on many women. Women's hemlines go up and down. The width of men's ties changes every few years. Bell-bottom pants are "out" now, and so on. Popular culture lasts a very short time.

The oldest kind of culture, however, is folk culture. Folk culture is *traditional* culture. It is the third kind of culture in Kentucky and the rest of the United States. We learn folk culture from our families, friends, fellow workers, and others around us. Often we do not know we are learning folk culture. We just soak it up as we grow and live our everyday lives.

Our lives are full of folk culture. An example of folk culture is called folklore. Folklore includes such things as folk speech, proverbs, riddles, folk songs, folktales, and many other things in our everyday lives. Folklore even includes traditional food recipes. For example, a Kentucky woman puts cornbread in her Christmas dressing. An Illinois woman probably does not.

Folk culture and folklore are like what Abraham Lincoln said about this country. That is, folk culture and folklore are of the people, by the people, and for the people. Anything that is passed down as a tradition from one generation to the next is usually folklore. All our unwritten, oral, traditional, local, "the way we do it around here" ways of life are folklore. This book will help you to learn more about Kentucky folklore.

All three cultures—elite, popular, and folk—affect our daily lives. The total of all three cultures is the total of who and what we are as cultural human beings. In this book, we will look at some of the folk cultural characteristics of Kentuckians.

Folk Speech

People sometimes say Kentuckians talk funny. What they don't know is that Kentuckians may think outsiders sound funny. The truth is, neither talks funny. They just talk in a different way.

For example, the common term "you-all" is not just a Kentucky term. "You-all" is heard all over the South. Sometimes even people outside the South say it. As far as grammar is concerned, "you-all" is perfectly correct. But people in different places say "you-all" in different ways. In some places, people stress both words the same—*"you-all."* In other places people jam both words together—"y'all" or even "yawl."

People say, "That's the way we say it around here"; and they're right. People say "you-all" the right way for them. The way you have learned to say something in your local folk culture is the proper one. We have to respect everybody's right to be different.

The term "you-all" is a part of our dialect. Our dialect includes the words we use and the way we say them. Our dialect is part of our folk culture. We all learn our dialect from our family and friends while we are growing up.

We do not learn our dialect on purpose, however. Children do not *try* to talk like their families or friends. Most of the time they do not even know that they are learning to talk a certain way. The way people talk just seems natural to them.

We learn a lot of folk culture in an informal, casual, natural process. We soak it up; nobody really teaches us. You cannot soak up folk culture unless you grow up with it. You have to have folk culture passed on to you every day from everybody around you as you are growing up. The way we talk, our dialect, is learned or passed on in a natural, traditional way.

On the other hand, we learn elite culture in schools or other official and formal ways. Some people believe there is just one correct, or elite culture, way to speak. When teachers try to get us to speak the "correct" way, they are teaching us elite culture. A teacher is supposed to teach elite culture. Therefore, teachers often try to get their Kentucky students to stop using "you-all" and other local folk culture ways of speaking.

We need to know all sorts of ways to speak. If you gave a public talk, you would not speak the same way you do when you are at home. A public talk is elite culture. Speaking at home is usually folk culture. Both kinds of speech are perfectly correct, in their place.

For example, a Kentuckian might say to his wife, very proudly, "I ain't never owed nothin' to nobody at no time!" Another Kentuckian, while asking a bank president for a loan, might say "I have never been in debt in my entire life."

Both are saying the same thing. They are just saying it in different ways. The first way is folk speech or what we learn at home and from our friends. The second way is elite culture speech or how we learn to talk in school.

Even if those two Kentuckians say the same thing, the way they sound might be different. The sound of both Kentucky speakers would also be part of their Kentucky dialect. No matter what they say or how they sound, one way is not better than the other. Each way is what is called for at the time. Therefore, every dialect has its proper place.

So dialect is why Kentuckians sound different to other people. Dialect is also why other people sound different to Kentuckians. Even Kentuckians from different parts of the state do not sound the same when they talk. People from the next county might sound different to you, and you might sound different to them. Both of you might say words a different way. Both of you might have different words or sayings.

In addition to "you-all," some Kentuckians use other folk pronouns such as "you'n," "her'n," "his'n," "our'n," "us'uns," "we'uns," "you'uns," "this'un," and "that'un."

You can also hear colorful folk adjectives in Kentucky. A number of Kentuckians use interesting adjectives to compare things. Some examples are "more happier," "worser," "more higher," "more better," "most highest," and "welcomer."

Some Kentuckians use a special adjective that adds an "-est." For instance, a young Kentucky lad might say, "She's the kissingest gal I ever did see!" It would be a compliment to call a man the "God-fearin'est" man you ever "knowed."

Kentuckians use many folk nouns, such as folk names. The U.S. Board of Geographic Names says that most names of places in the United States are folk names. Kentucky probably has even more folk place names than most other states.

Let's look at some of the more colorful names of Kentucky places. In far Western Kentucky there is a place called Monkey's Eyebrow in Ballard County. At least four places in the state are called Needmore. I heard that the one in Nelson County was called

Needmore because they need more people. There's a place on the Green River called Napper's Rollover. That's where they rolled logs over a hill down to the river in early logging days.

A good example of folk speech differences is the way different Kentuckians say the name of Kentucky's largest city. Many natives of Louisville say "Louavul." (There is even a bumper sticker that says "I love Louavul.") Kentuckians from other parts of the state usually say "LOUIEville." Some people, especially non-Kentuckians, even say "LEWISville."

While we are talking about folk names, we should look at some nicknames, which are also part of folk culture. In his book *The Kentucky,* historian Tom Clark talks about the nicknames of some of the Combs family in Eastern Kentucky. It seems that many Combses have the same first name. People have to give them nicknames to know which ones they are talking about. For instance, many Combses are named Jerry. So there is "Tight" Jerry, "Loose" Jerry, "Free" Jerry, "Round" Jerry, "Slow" Jerry, "Chunky" Jerry, "Short" Jerry, and "Beetle Nose" Jerry. Also, a Kentucky father and son with the same name will often be called "Big" and "Little" Bill, Jim, or whatever.

Even family names (surnames) usually have some folk culture meaning. For instance, if your name is

Smith your ancestors were probably blacksmiths or tinsmiths or worked with their hands in some way. My name goes all the way back to Anglo-Saxon times in England. It originally was Aelfwig and meant elk warrior. Your name probably has an interesting meaning, too. By learning how to read you will be able to look up the meaning of your name.

Some Kentuckians add "-ie" to many first given names, or even proper names. So, for example, Martha becomes Marthie, Bertha becomes Berthie, and Indiana becomes Indianie. Nearly every given name also has folk culture meaning. Martha means lady, and Bertha means bright. Many Kentucky men are named Homer, which means blind one. The name Homer comes from the famous blind Greek poet who wrote about the ancient city of Troy.

Other early Kentucky names show that the first Kentucky settlers had a lot of "book-larnin'." They named their children after poets and other writers. This shows that not all early settlers in Kentucky were uneducated people, as some people claim.

Many early Kentuckians named their children after people in the Bible, and many still do. A favorite old Kentucky name is Jethro. It comes from old Hebrew and means abundance. Many Kentuckians say your first name is your Christian name.

Kentuckians have always been religious. There are many folk terms about religion. For example, no one wants to be a "backslider" (a sinner). There are many "hardshell" (primitive) Baptists in Kentucky. A Kentucky minister gets "the calling" to become a preacher. His congregation attends church in their "Sunday-go-to-meetin'-clothes." "Old Ned" and "Old Scratch" are terms for the Devil. To escape the Devil one has to "get saved." Part of being saved is having a "baptizin'," especially before you have a "funeralizin." After you are saved and "git religion," you have been "borned again." From then on you will "try to do right" and live "accordin' to the Word." On "Judgmint Day" you want to be found in "that 'ol time religion" so you can go to the "Glory Land." There are many more religious terms.

Church bulletins often contain humorous folk expressions. Here are some announcements from different Kentucky churches: "Next week during the Ladies' Missionary Society meeting Mrs. Talbot will sing 'Put me in My Little Bed,' with the Pastor accompanying her." "Because this is Easter Sunday, we will ask Mrs. Anderson to come forward and lay an egg on the altar." "We will close the service with 'Little Drops of Water'; one of the men will start quietly and then the rest of the congregation will join in." "The ladies of the church have cast off clothing of every kind, and they can be seen in the church basement on Wednesday afternoon." "Next Sunday we will have meetings at both the North and South ends of the church. Children will be baptized at both ends."

Though most Kentuckians are religious, many misquote the *Bible*. Such misquotes are folk expressions. "Money is the root of all evil" is the misquote you hear most. The correct quote is "The love of money is the root of all evil." "Cleanliness is next to Godliness" is not even in the *Bible*.

Two other Kentucky folk religious terms are "preacher-man" and "church-house." In Kentucky folk speech there are many compound words. Other examples are "widder-woman," "pasture-field," "ham-meat," "biscuit-bread," "friendly-like," "bed-blanket," "brought-on" (bought at a store), "shin-bone," "eye-ball," "grass-widder" (divorcee), "rock-cliff," "rifle-gun," "nurse-woman," "nose-hole," "puny-lookin'," and "tooth-dentist."

The names of many ailments and diseases are treated a special way in Kentucky folk speech. People will often say they have *the* illness or disease. For example, people will say they have *the* asthmie, or *the* croup, or *the* fever, or *the* pneumonia, or *the* rheumatiz. To tell someone he or she doesn't look well, some Kentuckians might say, "You look like you got th' punies.' " A reply might be, "I reckon as how

I have." You could also say, "You look kinda peak-
ed." Then they might reply, "Well, I have been kinda
poorly." If someone is very ill, a Kentuckian might
say, seriously, "He's real bad off."

In other Kentucky folk speech, verbs often take
the "- ed" form of the past tense. For example,
talking about a vegetable from her garden, a
Kentuckian might say, "I growed it." In the elite
culture speech we learn in school, the same thing
would be, "I grew it." Or, if asked about his
neighbor, a Kentuckian might say, "I knowed him for
a long time." In elite culture or school speech, it
would be, "I have known him for a long time."

Kentucky folk speech has a special form of the
"-ed" past tense verb. Some Kentuckians often
change the "-ed" of past tense verbs to "-t." For
instance, in early days someone found a carving on a
Kentucky tree. It was about Daniel Boone killing a
bear. It said: "D. Boone kilt a bar." The same
pattern exists today. A man might say, "That cat *spilt*
that turpentine all over the chair and just *ruint* it."
His wife might add, "Yes, and it like-to *scairt* me to
death when he done it too!"

Kentucky folk speech also has many other colorful
verbs and terms. For example, some Kentuckians say,
"I'll carry that sack." Others say, "I'll tote that poke"
or "I'll pack it."

Some Kentuckians use "carry" to mean a car ride. For instance, a Kentuckian might ask his friend, "Would you carry me uptown?" His friend might reply, "I don't care to," which means yes, the friend does not object to taking him to town.

"Fixin'-to" is a commonly used special term meaning to get ready to do something. A rural Kentucky man might say, "My old lady's done hid my shine on me, but I'm a-fixin' to go find it."

The "a-" form folk preposition is also common. A man might ask his friend, "Well, where was ya at a-Saturday night? I betcha warn't home a-bed." He might reply, "Well no, I'll tell ya, jest a-tween us two, I was a-dancin' myself to death."

Kentucky folk speech also has different folk vowels. For example, Kentuckians often say the vowel "i" so that it sounds like an "a." A man might say, "Git yur tar arn (tire iron) and we'll change yur tar." Also, the "far house" (fire house) is where you keep "far trucks" to put out "fars."

Many Kentuckians say the word "it" by putting an "h-" in front of it—for example, "Hit'll be a cold day in July before I do that." Or to state that something doesn't make any difference, someone might say, "Hit don't matter," "Hit don't make no never mind," or "Hit don't make no difference nohow."

The folk speech expression "don't make no" is called a double negative. Elite culture considers double negatives to be wrong. In elite culture, the same thing would be stated "doesn't make any." But hundreds of years ago in England, the double negative was considered correct speech. This shows that what is considered correct changes over the years. It also shows that Kentuckians' folk culture, like folk culture everywhere, does not change much. In fact, some college teachers believe that Kentuckians' folk speech is pretty close to the way people talked in England hundreds of years ago. Folk culture prefers the traditional ways of doing everything, including talking.

Because outsiders have made fun of them, some Kentuckians have two kinds of speech. One is for strangers, and the other is for use at home or with friends. An outsider might never hear many of the examples given here. It's too bad that folk speech and other differences tend to keep us from being close to other people. Instead, folk culture differences should make us more interesting to each other.

Folk culture differences explain why a Kentucky second grade student told his new teacher from Massachusetts, "You sure do talk funny." He had never heard anyone from outside his Kentucky county speak. So to him she sounded funny. If he and the rest of her students sounded funny to her, she would not say so. That would not be polite. She knew why she and her students sounded funny to each other. She knew that her culture was different from her students' culture—not better, not worse, just different.

When we understand culture, we get to be more like that schoolteacher. We begin to accept all kinds of different people for what they are. We see that they are not better or worse than we are. They are just different from us, just as we are different from them. That makes us feel better about them. Then we are more comfortable around people who are different from us.

Understanding people and their culture in this way makes us better human beings. It makes us more accepting of all sorts of differences. Most of us prefer our own culture. But we should realize that no one culture is best for everybody.

Proverbs and
Other Expressions

Kentuckians have many interesting proverbs and folk expressions. A proverb is a traditional folk saying that is supposed to contain the wisdom of ages of experience. Many of them are in the *Bible*, in the Book of Proverbs.

People usually say a proverb to someone to be helpful, but using proverbs is really like preaching. That is, a proverb is used to correct or warn someone about something. In a way, then, to tell others a proverb is like meddling in their business or giving smug advice.

For example, one of your friends is on the outs with his wife and has said some mean things to her. You might tell him the proverb "Men should be careful about makin' wimmen cry, 'cause God counts their tears." Your friend might tell you that his wife was mean to him first and say, "What's good fur th' goose is good fur th' gander." So you can actually argue with proverbs.

Some interesting proverbs often heard in Kentucky are "Don't count yer chickens afore they're hatched" ; "He's eatin' ham-meat on sow-belly wages"; "She's a honey but th' bees don't know it"; "If you lay down

Holy Family School

with dogs you're gonna git up with fleas"; "That ol' dog won't hunt"; "Root hog or die"; "Two head's better'n one even if one's a punkin head"; "Don't chew yer baccer twice"; and "Ya kaint make a silk purse out'a a sow's ear."

Kentuckians have even more proverbial sayings and other folk expressions than they do proverbs. There are sayings for nearly every situation. For example, when referring to a gossip someone might say, "I believe she'd talk about her Savior if'n he was here on earth" or "A dog that will bring a bone will take one." A nervous person is "jest like a fly on a manure pile" or "as nervous as a long-tailed cat in a room full 'a' rockin' chairs."

Kentuckians do not like stuck-up people. Here are two sayings for such people: "His folks are like taters: the best uns are buried" and "Preachers, lawyers, and buzzard eggs: there's been more hatched than ever come to perfection."

A mean woman is "so mean she'd take pennies offen a dead man's eyes and kick him for not courtin' her." About her husband, they might say, "The Devil owed him a debt and paid him off with her." About an argument they had, someone could say, "Why she cussed him 'til a fly wouldn't light on him."

About someone who drinks too much, it is said,

"He'd cross hell on a rotten rail to get a drink a' likker." Kentuckians also laugh at themselves a lot. A homely man might say, "I was hidin' behind th' door when th' looks was passed out." Or a sad man might say, "I feel like th' hind wheels of hard times." A contrary man might say he's "muley-hawed."

The following is an example of how folk speech and expressions might be used in everyday situations. A woman might say: "I swan, I ain't seen nothin' like it in all my born days. Here th' preacher's a'comin' fur supper and hit's a'snowin' shoe-mouth deep. And all we's got is miner's strawberries ta put on th' table. And no doubt him expectin' ta eat enuf to feel fatter'n a tick on a dog's neck. And lookie here, you younguns hasn't even redd up th' house yit."

"Shoe-mouth deep," of course, means as deep as the top of your shoes. To "redd up" means to tidy up the house. "Miner's strawberries" is the humorous term for beans. In Kentucky folk speech, "supper" usually means the evening meal. Except in urban areas, Kentuckians usually do not use the word "lunch." Instead, "dinner" is what most Kentuckians call the noon meal.

Kentuckians have many folk terms for food and its use. Some call food "vittles" or "grub." When cooking, some Kentucky women often say they're "fixin' a mess" of greens. You tell a guest, "Set down ritecheer and make out a meal fur yurself."

That meal might include "a mess a' poke sallat greens"; "leather britches"; "shuckie beans"; "chitlins"; "'maters"; "'taters"; "hog meat" or "cow meat"; "corn pone," "biscuit- bread," "johnnycake" or "hoecake"; "speargrass" (asparagus); "'lasses"; "yarbs"; "cow-juice"; and "pie-plant" (rhubarb). Dessert might be "burries" or "stack cake."

Before the meal, one of the people might look at the table and say, "I'm so hungry I could eat a sow and her six pigs." After a fine meal, the guest might say, "I'm as full as a hog under an acorn tree." After dinner, the men might sneak off and have a drink of homemade "alkeyhaul" (or "shine"). Later the men might go to the local country store and have a "sodie pop" and a "Moon Pie" or a "chaw" from an "auger" of "tabacer."

The most common Kentucky folk expressions are probably traditional proverbial comparisons to everyday things. They can be applied to almost anybody or anything. Here are some examples: "ugly as homemade sin"; "naked as a peeled apple"; "independent as a hog on ice"; "busy (or nervous) as a cow's tail in flytime"; "nervous as a rabbit's nose" or "nervous as an old hen with one chick"; "mean as a (rattle) snake"; "no more hips'n snake"; "takes to it like a pig takes to slop"; "no more use fur that'n a hog needs sidepockets"; "live so fur back in th' holler they got ta pipe in daylight"; "sharp as a tack and twice as flatheaded"; "crooked as a dog's hind leg an' twice as dirty"; and "thicker'n fiddlers in hell."

Some of these expressions have a lot of meaning and history behind them. For example, the last expression, "thicker'n fiddlers in hell," is very old. It comes from a time when many Kentuckians felt that drinking alcohol was sinful (and many still believe that). Anyway, the saying does not mention alcohol. It's about fiddlers, and it says many fiddlers go to hell. That's because most of the heavy drinking in earlier times was done at dances where fiddlers often played all night. Also, fiddlers were often the ones who gave out the alcohol at such affairs. That old saying is really about drinking too much and not about playing the fiddle. Many Kentucky folk expressions have similar interesting histories.

In the hilly parts of Kentucky, people often use funny expressions to talk about how hilly and poor the land is. A man might joke that his farm is "so steep I can look down the chimly and see what my old lady's fixin' fur supper." Another farmer might say, "My land's so hilly I'm askeered a fallin' out–a my field and breakin' my neck." Hill farmers joke that "land's so pore it wouldn't raise a fight" or "so pore a rabbit's gotta carry his dinner when he goes acrosst it." Many people joke that Kentuckians born and raised in the hills have one leg shorter than the other "so's they can walk standin' up straight."

Many Kentuckians from rural areas are tall and skinny, so there are a number of skinny comparison jokes. I have a thin friend who says, "I'm so skinny I can take shelter under the clothesline when it rains and not get wet." He also says, "I'm so skinny I just turn sideways to hide from my wife."

Kentucky folk expressions sum up what everybody knows or thinks in a catchy, funny way. They are used in many situations.

Riddles and Puzzles

A riddle is another kind of traditional folklore Kentuckians like to use. Riddles are usually humorous and are often told as a game. The idea is to see if you can outwit someone by asking a riddle he or she can't answer.

Before the arrival of TV, radio, and the movies, adult Kentuckians told riddles for fun. But riddles also are a form of teaching and mental exercise. Today, riddles are usually told by school children. Even children's riddles still teach. You can really sharpen your wits and mind by guessing riddles.

There are all kinds of riddles. Some riddles are old, but people make up new riddles all the time. One of the older traditional riddles in Kentucky is the so-called riddle of the Sphinx. It is not just a Kentucky riddle. People all over the world know and use this riddle: "What goes on four legs in the mornin', two legs in the afternoon, and three legs at night?" The answer is "man." He crawls when he's a baby, walks on two legs when grown, and uses a cane when he's old.

Kentuckians have many riddles about animals. "Why does a little pig eat so much?" is an example. The answer is "to make himself inta a big fat hog." This shows that the answers to most riddles are truths or facts everyone should know. The riddle just presents these facts in a funny way.

Here are a few favorite Kentucky riddles and their answers:

What's got eyes but no head, and a head but no eyes? (Answer: needles 'n pins)

How can ya keep from gettin' that run-down feelin'? (Answer: look both ways afore crossin' the road)

How's a hen on a fence like a penny? (Answer: got a tail on one side 'n a head on t'other)

What's the reddest side of an apple? (Answer: the outside)

What can a man give a woman but can't give a man? (Answer: his name)

Why don't women go bald as soon as men? (Answer: 'cause they wear their hair longer)

What goes up and down th' road all day 'n' sticks its tongue out from under th' bed at night? (Answer: a wagon)

Hundreds of years ago, some riddles were meant to be so hard that nobody could answer them except the person who told them. Some people call these "neck" riddles, because they could save your neck. In some places custom ruled that if a person was condemned to hang, he or she was allowed to ask a riddle. If no one could guess the correct answer, the person's neck (life) would be spared.

You can still hear some of those old neck riddles in Kentucky. Early settlers brought them from Europe and Britain. People just kept saying them, but Americans did not use them to save their necks! Here is one that is popular in Kentucky.

Love I sit, Love I stand,
Love I hold in my right hand,
Love I see in yonder tree.
Unriddle this riddle, and you can hang me.

There is a story behind this neck riddle: The man about to be hanged had a dog named Love. When the dog died, he skinned it because he loved it so much. He wanted to keep whatever he could of the dog. For luck, he put a piece of the skin in his hip pocket, a piece in his shoe, a piece in his glove, and tacked a piece up in an old oak tree in his yard.

Many Kentucky riddles are like the neck riddles. They are puzzle riddles. For example: "I rode across London Bridge, yet I walked." Answer: "I rode. My dog ["Yet I"] walked behind me." This is a trick riddle. Trick riddles are popular in Kentucky. Here is the oldest and most popular trick riddle in Kentucky. It probably came from England.

When I was agoin' to St. Ives,
I met up with a man that had seven wives,
And each of them wives had seven sacks,
And each of them sacks had seven cats,
And each of them cats had seven kittens.
Now, kittens, cats, sacks, and wives,
How many was agoin' to St. Ives?
    [Answer: one]

Many Kentucky puzzle riddles are about farm topics. Here is a good example: "Yonder sits a green house. Inside th' green house there's a white house. Inside th' white house there's a red house. Inside th' red house there's a whole passel a little black 'n' white men." Answer: a watermelon.

Some of these puzzle riddles are pretty hard. Here is one of the harder ones popular in Kentucky. "There's these here three men. One weighs two hundred pounds. The other two weigh one hundred pounds apiece. They got to git acrosst th' river. There's a boat there, but it'll jest carry two hundred pounds. How they gonna git acrosst?" Answer: First the two skinny men get in and go across. Then one comes back. Then the two hundred pound man goes across alone. Then the one skinny man goes back and gets the other skinny man.

Riddles like these make you think. Also, you have to use math and other skills to figure them out. You can actually learn by doing riddles, and you can have fun at the same time.

A favorite traditional folk puzzle or riddle is the tongue-twister. Tongue-twisters are not really puzzles or riddles, but they work like them. You have to figure out how to say them without making a mistake. Here are two of the better traditional tongue-twisters in Kentucky.

Peter Piper picked a peck of pickled peppers.
A peck of pickled peppers Peter Piper picked.
If Peter Piper picked a peck of pickled peppers,
Where is the peck of pickled peppers Peter Piper picked?

A big black bug bit a big black bear on the end of his big black nose and made the big black bear bleed blood.

A rebus is another kind of puzzle some Kentuckians like. A rebus combines words, letters, and numbers to say something. You have to figure out what it says. A rebus often rhymes. The following is probably the favorite rebus in Kentucky:

	Answer:
2 Y's U R	Too wise you are
2 Y's U B	Too wise you be
I C U R	I see you are
2 Y's 4 ME	Too wise for me

Another favorite rebus of both children and adults is:

	Answer:
M R Boy Puppies	Them are boy puppies
M R Not Boy Puppies	Them are not boy puppies
O S A R	Oh yes they are
C M P N	See 'em peein'
L I B	Well, I be
M *R* Boy Puppies!	Them *are* boy puppies!

Other riddles also rhyme. Here are two similar rhyming ones.

Round as a biscuit, deep as a cup,
Ohio River can't fill it up. [Answer: a sieve]

Round as a biscuit, thin as a knife,
Guess this riddle and I'll be your wife. [Answer: a dime]

Like all riddles, these compare things. In each one you have to guess what's being compared to a round biscuit. Riddles teach how language can be used to describe the same thing in many different ways. Anyone who is good at riddles should also be good at using language in different ways.

Because we have fun when we do riddles, we are not aware that we are also learning about language. Because many riddles are rhymes also makes them fun. Rhymes teach us about language. Many other kinds of Kentucky folklore also use rhymes.

Folk Rhymes

Some of the first rhymes Kentuckians use are children's rhymes. Here are two versions of an all-time favorite:

Roses are red,	Roses are red,
Violets are blue,	Violets are blue,
Sugar is sweet,	Your mother's pretty,
And so are you.	But what happened to you?

There are many versions of this "roses are red" rhyme. Many of them are put in school yearbooks, autograph books, and so forth.

Kentucky yearbooks and autograph books are full of folk rhymes. Here are three favorites of Kentucky children:

I seen you in the ocean,
I seen you in the sea,
I seen you in the bathtub,
Oops, pardon me!

Remember north,
Remember south,
Remember me,
And my big mouth.

After you get married,
And your husband gets cross,
Hit him with a broom,
To show him who's boss!

Like all folklore, these rhymes teach as well as entertain. The first two teach modesty and humility. The third one says something funny about the way married people are supposed to act.

As part of their everyday lives, Kentucky children also use rhymes for folk games (such as "fox and geese"), jumping rope, taunts and teases, and other activities.

Here is a favorite Kentucky children's teasing rhyme:

Billy and Annie sittin' in a tree,
K-i-s-s-i-n-g!
First comes LOVE, then comes MARRIAGE,
Then comes Annie pushin' a BABY CARRIAGE!

Although children use this rhyme to tease, it also teaches. The order of events in the rhyme is just as it is supposed to happen in real life—love, marriage, babies—in that order. Like this rhyme, a lot of folklore teaches morals.

A parody is another favorite kind of rhyme. A parody is formed when you take a well-known rhyme, song, or saying and make fun of it by substituting new words. For example, here is a parody of "The Star-Spangled Banner," our national anthem:

Ohhh say can you see,
Any bedbugs on me?

If you can, take a few,
'Cause I got 'em from you.

The more serious something is, the more likely children will make a parody of it. Children use parodies to rebel against adult authority. They also use them to show that they are not impressed with serious adult subjects. That's why they made a parody of our national anthem. Here's another Kentucky parody:

Now I lay me down to sleep,
Bag 'a' green apples at my feet.
If I die b'fore I wake,
You'll know it was a tummie ache.

This parody allows the child to make fun of the prayer. It also allows the child to say something that is on the child's mind. In this case, the child's tummy concerns him or her more than praying to bless all his or her brothers, sisters, and other family members, as parents usually expect.

Children in Kentucky also have parodies of many commercial slogans and rhymes. Here is an example:

Sani-Flush, Sani-Flush,
It'll clean your teeth without a brush!

These parodies allow children to show that they are not taken in by know-it-all and preachy commercials.

In Kentucky, you can find a parody for almost any serious topic. Even Kentucky adults have parodies. Here are two of them:

The Government is my Shepherd, I need not work.
It encourageth me to lie down on a good job.
It leadeth me beside the still factories.
It destroyeth my initiative, and confiscateth my
      earnings.
It leadeth me in the path of a parasite, for politics'
      sake.
Yea, though I walk through the valley of deficit
      spending,
I will fear no evil, for the Government is with me.
Its Social Security and its price supports, they
      comfort me.
It promiseth an economic utopia, and
      appropriateth all the earnings of my
      grandchildren.
It filleth my head with the false security of a
      dream world,
Until my inefficiency runneth over.
Surely the Government will care for me all the
      days of my life,
And I shall dwell in a fool's paradise forever.

This is, of course, a parody of the Twenty-third Psalm. It first appeared September 18, 1977, in *The Scraper*, the magazine of the Kentucky Association of Highway Contractors. It has been copied, sent,

40

and read all over Kentucky. One of my students gave me a copy of it. Many parodies like this are copied and passed around all over the United States, even the world.

Here's another parody of the Twenty-third Psalm about Richard M. Nixon:

Nixon is my Shepherd, I shall not want. He leadeth me by the still factories. He restoreth my doubt in the Republican Party. He giveth me to the path of unemployment for the party's sake. I do not fear evil for Thou art against me. Thou anointest my wages with freezes so my expenses runneth over my income. Surely poverty and hard living shall follow the Republican Party and I will live in a rented house forever.
P.S. I am glad I am an American. I am glad I am free. But I wish I was a little dog and Nixon was a tree.

Both parodies are protests about politics. The average person in Kentucky, or elsewhere, has no chance to talk to people in Washington. Even if he or she did, it probably would not make any difference. So traditional parodies such as these give the common people a chance to say how they feel about important things, such as politics. Thus, parodies like this are the average person's voice or way to lobby against politics he or she doesn't like.

Other funny and sad traditional rhymes are found on gravestones. Any writing on a gravestone is called an epitaph. Epitaphs are as old as human beings. Many epitaphs have rhymed traditional messages.

Now listen my children as you pass by,
As you are now, so once was I.
As I am now, so you must be.
So dry up your tears,
And follow me.

This old traditional epitaph is found all over the country. It soberly calls us to our graves, reminding us that we are mortal. That serves to make us humble. So the epitaph teaches a serious and eternal truth. Because it rhymes, it also amuses us. Because it charms us with its rhyming wit, we are even more likely to remember the epitaph's sober message about death. Here is a similar, unrhymed, one:

Shall	We	All	Die?
We	Shall	Die	All!
All	Die	Shall	We?
Die	All	We	Shall!

This is another old epitaph found on gravestones all over the country. Like much of our folklore, it probably came from Britain. Any way you read the epitaph, its gloomy message is the same: we are all going to die.

Some epitaphs, however, are more
serious.

It was a cough that carried him
It was his coffin they carried him

Since I have been so quickly done for,
I wonder what I was begun for. [Infant epitaph

Beneath this stone our baby lies.
It neither cries or hollers.
It lived but one and twenty days,
And cost us forty dollars. [Infant epitaph]

Of course, no matter how funny, epitaphs are also sad
and sobering. It is a testimony to the human spirit
that we can find room for humor even in such sad
times. People say that our sense of humor is one of
the saving graces of Americans. Maybe we *need* to
have humor, especially in trying times, such as death.

Nearly all traditions about an event such as death
are called folk customs. Kentucky has so many
traditional folk customs, folk beliefs, and
superstitions that you could fill several books listing
them. In our limited space, we will discuss some of
the more interesting ones.

oms, Beliefs,
d Superstitions

Since we have just talked about epitaphs, let's talk about death customs in Kentucky. Stopping your car for a funeral procession is a widespread Kentucky folk custom to show respect. No law says you must pull over and stop for a funeral procession, but nearly everyone does. This shows the power of traditional folk customs in our lives. We obey such unwritten rules just as if they were the official laws of elite culture. Some Kentuckians also follow many other folk customs about death.

For example, some people stop all the clocks in the house when someone dies. Some people cover all pictures and mirrors or turn them toward the wall. People say they do these things to prevent other deaths in the family. Kentucky has many death superstitions and omens.

Death comes in threes in a congregation.
A wild bird in the house means someone's going to die.
A dog howling three nights in a row means death is near.
If you get shingles all around your body, you'll die.
If you sneeze, cover your mouth and say the Lord's

name, or you'll lose your soul out of your mouth and die.

If two women help a third one get dressed, the youngest of the three will die.

There are thousands of superstitions like these in Kentucky.

An old Kentucky funeral custom is to put coins on the dead person's eyes. This custom is thousands of years old. Back then people believed that the dead person's soul had to cross a river. The money was to pay for the ferry ride to the other side.

If there are beehives nearby, some Kentuckians believe that you must go and tell the bees about the death. If you don't, the dead person will not have a safe trip to the other side. The bees will leave if they are not told about the death.

The original purpose for the traditional folk custom of having flowers at a funeral was to hide the smell of the dead body! That was before embalming. Today, flowers are just nice. But many Kentuckians will not bring home flowers from a funeral for fear they will cause another death.

In earlier days, it was the custom to "set up with" or keep a "death watch" with the body, which usually was kept in the home before burial. Friends and relatives did this to show respect for the deceased and to protect the body until burial.

"Decoration Day" is the term many Kentuckians use for the folk custom the rest of the country calls Memorial Day. In some parts of Kentucky people have an all-day religious service on Decoration Day. It usually includes "dinner on the ground," the picnic part of the all-day service. The custom of the all-day service started many years ago.

Back then, when someone died there was often no preacher available. Many early preachers rode circuits, serving a wide area on horseback. Sometimes, the preacher came only once each year. So people would have a service for events that had happened during the past year, including a memorial service for those who had died. Such services would often last all day, especially if a number of people had died. Also, a folk belief says that the first one to leave a funeral service will be the next one to die. So not too many people wanted to leave early.

Other Kentucky folk customs and festivals include the stir-off in the fall, when sorghum molasses is made by grinding the cane with a mule-driven mill; the traditional quiltin'-bee, when neighborhood women get together to talk, eat, and make beautiful Kentucky quilts (the best quilter is supposed to get sixteen stitches to the inch!); the old-fashioned house-raisin' or barn-raisin', when neighbors pitch in and build a barn in a day (the women always serve traditional food to the workers); corn-shuckin's, log-rollin's, threshin's, hog-butcherin's, and other group "workin's" where friends, relatives, and neighbors help one another; the old-fashioned "pound-party," where everyone brings a pound of food for a missionary couple going off, for a new preacher, for a new neighbor, or for people in need; the traditional shivaree, or chivaree, when friends and relatives "sing" to newlyweds on their wedding night with cowbells, shotgun blasts, banging pots and pans, and so on (the custom of decorating the newlyweds' car is a modern version of the old shivaree); the widespread "tooth-fairy" custom for making the loss of children's teeth less painful; and the folk customs of cock-fighting and fox and coon hunting, when friends use the hunting trip mainly to talk and tell stories.

There are thousands of folk beliefs and superstitions in Kentucky. Though we don't have space to discuss them, here are some Kentucky folk beliefs. Most folk beliefs concern either the supernatural or questions that science and medicine or religion do not answer to suit us. For example, here are a few Kentucky weather beliefs.

If hornets nest close to the ground, winter'll be cold.
If the corns on your toes ache, it's goin' ta rain.

47

Heavy fur on an animal means a cold winter.
When camphor rises in a bottle, it means rain.
It'll snow in May if it thunders in February.

Elite culture's scientific method of weather prediction
is not exact. Many people think folk weather beliefs
are as good as the weather bureau's elite culture
attempts.

Here are just a few of the thousands of Kentucky
folk cures.

To cure hiccups, you put a brown bag over your
head.
To get rid of warts, rub 'em with an old rotten
dishrag an' bury the dishrag when th' moon's
full.
Blow warm pipe smoke in your ear to cure an
earache.
You cure measles with a tea made out of sheep
droppings.
Mare's milk will cure th' whoopin' cough.
Ta cure a baby's thrash, you got ta git a "thrash
doctor" ta blow in his mouth.
Rub gunpowder and buttermilk on poison ivy.
Use lots a' cow manure on a stone bruise or for
freckles.

These are quite different from cures prescribed by
a medical doctor. People try folk cures when elite
culture medicine does not work or when elite medical
science does not think the problems are important,

such as freckles, colds, or warts. (There are also folk cures for animal ailments.)

Here are some Kentucky superstitions about bad luck.

If a bride makes her own clothes, it's bad luck.
It's bad luck to kiss a girl behind the ear.
If you kill a cat, it'll haunt you all your life.
It's bad luck to tell a dream or sing before
   breakfast.

Here are some Kentucky folk beliefs about good luck.

It's good luck to have your family cat at your
   wedding.
It's good luck to put your clothes on wrongside
   out if you do it by mistake.
On Friday the thirteenth wear odd shoes for good
   luck.
It's good luck to carry a buckeye in your pocket.

Here are some other Kentucky folk beliefs.

The first night you sleep under a new quilt, you
   will dream of your true love.
When you give a knife as a present, they have to
   pay you at least a penny for it, or it'll "cut"
   your friendship.
If two workers' tools hit while they're workin',
   they'll be doin' that same thing the same time
   next year.

Kentuckians have folk beliefs, folk cures, and superstitions for almost any topic. You might want to make a list of those that you and your family and friends know.

Folk Songs

A special Kentucky folk celebration is the Big Singing Day held at Benton on the last Sunday in May. This folk custom is over one hundred years old. People from all over the country gather together to sing religious songs. Singing folk songs of all kinds, religious or not, is a popular folk custom all over Kentucky.

Beyond any doubt, the most popular religious folk song in Kentucky is "Amazing Grace." Here is the first stanza.

A-maz-ing Grace, how sweet the sound,
That saved a wretch like me.
I once was lost, but now I'm found,
Was blind, but now I see.

Another popular religious folk song in Kentucky is "Precious Memories." Aunt Molly Jackson was a folksinger and a leader in the Kentucky coal mine union struggles. She made up a protest parody, a nonreligious song based on "Precious Memories." She called it "Dreadful Memories" and sang it to call attention to the troubles of the coal miners. A lot of folk songs have been used as protest songs all over the world. They have a powerful message. Here are two versions.

Original folk song:
Precious memories, unseen angels,
Sent from heaven to my soul,
How they linger ever near me,
And the sacred past unfold.

Chorus: Precious memories, how they linger
How they ever flood my soul.
In the stillness of the moonlight,
Precious sacred scenes unfold.

Precious Father, loving mother,
Fly across the lonely years,
And old home scenes of my childhood,
In blessed memory appear.

As I travel on life's pathway,
And know not what the years may hold,
As I ponder, hope grows fonder,
Precious memories flood my soul.

Aunt Molly's protest folk song:
Dreadful memories, how they linger,
Oh how they ever flood my soul.
Oh how the workers, and their children,
All died from hunger and from cold.

Oh hungry fathers, weary mothers,
Living in those dreadful shacks,
Little children, cold and hungry,
With no clothing on their backs.

Oh dreadful gun thugs and stool pigeons,

Always hanging around our door.
Oh what's the crime that we've committed?
Nothing, only that we're poor.

Oh those memories, how they haunt me,
And make me want to organize.
And make me want to help the workers,
And make them open up their eyes.

We will have to join the union,
They will help you find a why,
How to make a better living,
And for your work get decent pay.

This widespread protest folk song is still being sung today.

Kentuckians also have many nonreligious humorous or light-hearted folk songs. Probably the best example is "Cripple Creek."

Goin' up Cripple Creek,
Goin' in a run,
Goin' up Cripple Creek,
Ta have me a little fun.

Roll up my britches to my knees,
Wade up Cripple Creek when I please.
Gals up Cripple Creek 'bout half-grown,
Jump on th' boys like a dog on a bone!

Other topics of folk songs include terrible murders, sad love affairs, tragic accidents (such as

Casey Jones's), and any event of historical importance. Folk songs preserve historical events and tell the common people's version of that event.

Perhaps the folk song "Little Omie Wise" is the best example of a Kentucky folk song about a terrible murder.

Oh tell me no stories, and tell me no lies,
Just tell me the story of little Omie Wise.
I'll tell you no story and I'll tell you no lies,
But how she was tricked by John Lewis' lies. . . .

Omie and Lewis were lovers. The story goes on to tell how Omie was to meet Lewis and bring him some money. She couldn't get any money. So he killed her and threw her body into the river. He was caught, and he paid for the crime. This murder happened in North Carolina over 150 years ago.

"Little Omie Wise" is a folk ballad. A ballad is a song that tells a story, usually about a real event. Kentuckians still sing "Little Omie Wise." The story is timeless. It could happen to anyone, anytime, anywhere. That is usually true of folk ballad topics. Kentuckians also tell stories that are not sung. Such stories are called folktales.

Folktales

Probably the most popular kind of folktale in Kentucky is the joke. Here is a good example of a widespread joke.

Oncet there was this here lazy man a-layin' on th' river bank a- fishin'. His pole was stuck in th' bank so's he wouldn't have ta hold it. 'Long comes a preacher. Th' preacher sees there's a fish jest a- tuggin' at th' line. Preacher says, "Hey, you got a fish." Th' lazy man asks th' preacher ta haul th' fish in an' put some new bait on th' hook. Well th' preacher does that an' says, "You're so lazy. I'll bet your wife don't like your being lazy." Lazy man says he ain't married. Preacher says, "Well, maybe you ought to get married. It'd probably stop your being so lazy." Lazy man says, "Well maybe I ort ta. How about you findin' me a woman ta marry up with?" Preacher says, "Well, I believe I can." Lazy man says, "Good, can ya git me one that's done pregnant?"

Often the person telling this joke will end it by saying, "Now *that's* a lazy man!" This is a Kentucky favorite. While it's funny, the joke also teaches, like all folklore. The joke shows that we do not admire lazy people; we make fun of them.

Kentuckians also tell a lot of local legends, such

as a story about the town character, a bad accident or murder, or any unusual event. For instance, there are stories still told around Russellville about the time Jesse James was supposed to have robbed the bank there. Supposedly, Jesse's bullet hole is still in the bank wall. That's the way I heard it, anyway. Nearly all local people know a version of such folktales. Or they know at least a part of the story.

Some of these local legends can be gruesome.

Back years ago, a woman had a bad car wreck out on th' highway. She was pronounced dead at the scene. No one knew who she was. She didn't have no ID on her. They went on an' buried her in th' public graveyard. What they didn't know was she wasn't dead! She was jest in a deep coma an' couldn't move or talk or anything. After a while they found out who she was and her people came to take her back an' bury her in th' family graveyard. When they opened th' coffin there was scratches all over th' inside where she had come out of th' coma an' tried to git out. Her fingers had also been eaten off! She tried to stay alive by eatin' her own fingers!

Many people fear being buried alive. Stories like this let us release those fears through the story. The story also shows the strong human will to live, even when buried alive!

Another local legend teaches a different lesson.

Back a long time ago, there was some men settin'
up with a sick man. They started drinkin' 'shine,
an' even gave th' sick man some. Th' men fell
asleep, but it pepped up th' sick man an' he got up
an' went outside. When th' others woke up they
started huntin' for him an' found him down th'
road passed out. He was too big ta carry so they
drug him back home. When they got him home
they saw somethin' awful. They had drug th' sick
man's heels off! Th' next mornin' they told his
family that th' rats had got in his bed an' ate his
heels off.

Here we learn of the evils of drunkenness and failure
to do our duty. Many folktales have similar truths to
tell.

Some local folktales are about the supernatural.
For example, there are many ghost or "haint" tales
and stories about "spirits" who return to correct
something that was not right when they died.
Kentuckians tell a number of stories about the
returning spirit of a person who died by somehow
having his head cut off. Usually, as the story says,
the head couldn't be found and the body had to be
buried without it. The headless spirit returns to find
the head so it can rest in peace.

Many tales are about lovers being reunited. There

is a story told in Lexington about two lovers who were killed in a car wreck. He was Catholic. She was Protestant. In Lexington, the Catholic cemetery is across the road from the Protestant cemetery. The story says that you can see the boy's ghost go across the road to the girl's grave every year on the date of the wreck. Some stories tell of two lovers buried side by side. A rose briar grows out of each grave, and the briars and roses grow together. Stories like these lift our spirits and help to make us even closer to our loved ones.

Lots of tales tell of haunted houses and even of strange things going on in normal houses. For instance, many people tell stories about rocking chairs rocking with no one in them. Sometimes a piano will play, lights will come on, or doors will open, and no one is ever around when these things happen. Other stories tell how people hear voices or other human noises in the house; they can't explain these noises. Some modern tales are about UFOs and space creatures.

A favorite folktale of Kentucky men is the tall tale. It's also called a "fish story," a "yarn," a "liar's tale," or a "liar's bench story." That's because men often tell them while sitting around the courthouse, barber shop, or sale barn. The tales are usually about hunting, fishing, or some other outside activity. Here's a favorite example.

You 'member th' year of th' big blizzard? Well
I's out huntin' when it came up. I couldn't git
back home. I just found me a little ol' cave an'
holed up. I had my good ol' Kentucky long
rifle—muzzle loader, ya know. Well, pretty soon
here comes an ol' bear in the cave. I knowed I
was in trouble 'cause I was out'a shot pellets. So,
thinkin' real fast, I jest grabs me one 'a them
icicles a'hangin' down there in th' cave an' crams
it down th' barrel o' my ol' trusty long rifle. I
takes quick aim an' BLAM, I hit that ol' bear
right in th' head. Well, you know it FROZE him,
right on th' spot! Yessir! And ya know, I couldn't
git out 'a there till it thawed. An' ya know, when
it thawed that icicle in th' bear's head thawed too.
An' when it did that's what killed him—WATER ON
TH' BRAIN. Yessir, water on th' brain. Easiest
bear I ever got.

The more impossible these tall tales are, the better
people like them. Some men are known for their tall-
tale-telling ability.

This will have to end our discussion of Kentucky
folklore. There are many different kinds of Kentucky
folklore I haven't even mentioned. Anyway, to
appreciate folklore fully you have to see it and hear it
firsthand. I hope this book will help you to be more
aware of your own folklore. Maybe you will want to
use a tape recorder and record your Kentucky
folklore. If you do, send it to me!

About the Author

Gerald Alvey is an associate professor of English at the University of Kentucky, where he teaches folklore and folklife. His professional interests include the study of folklore in such diverse cultures as Appalachia and rural Kentucky, small towns, prisons, among Blacks, in rural Maine, in the business world, and among the Navajos, as well as folk art. His published writings include many articles and one book, *Dulcimer Maker: The Craft of Homer Ledford*. Works in progress deal with the folk school movement in Appalachia, the works of early Kentucky folklorist Josiah Combs, a biography of Henrietta Child (the "Story Lady" of Berea, Kentucky), and a study of knife-swapping in Appalachia.